Climb that Fence AND TAKE THAT Leap

Life lessons from my pet's antics

PHILIP JOHNSEY

ISBN-10: 1478200162
EAN-13: 9781478200161
Library of Congress Control Number: 2012912340
CreateSpace Independant Publishing Platform
North Charleston, South Carolina

Contents

Acknowledgements

The list is long, but I'd like to acknowledge my family for always being there to encourage and love me at the perfect time. To thank my beloved cat Keiko for sharing eighteen years of her life with me. I miss you but am glad you are no longer in pain. Thank you for many friends past and present who gave their support for my writings and provided a safe place to let it all out. And finally, I'd like to give a tremendous thank you to all the animal volunteers who tirelessly give of their time to save one more life.

Introduction

As an only child who grew up on a farm, I have a natural affinity for animals. Some of my fondest memories involve the miracle of life and the joy of companionship. I remember seeing a baby goat born and just a few minutes later take his first steps. I was amazed how quickly it could walk! Then there was the day I opened a big white box and saw hundreds of cotton soft yellow chicks going "peep, peep, peep." So humans come from storks and chickens from the mail?

Baby animals are always so cute and I always remember the litter of multicolor kittens following me everywhere and the variety of puppies who loved to play chase through the yard. These were my brothers and sisters. They never told on me, never took my stuff, and were always there no matter what. Although at times, I'd really wished they'd slept past 5 a.m.!!

Regardless of our individual upbringing, animals are always around us in some shape or form. Sometimes those forms are not what we like; such as snakes and skunks. Those of us with pets have a more intimate connection with animals, because our pets see us in all situations—awake, asleep, disheveled, happy, depressed, excited, and disappointed. How many times have you had a conversation out loud with yourself thinking the house was empty, when all along your pet was sitting on the bed? They truly hear it all and see it all.

With such a close connection to us, it's no surprise our pets can give us insights. Who better to help us than someone who knows us inside out? It'd be nice if they'd sit down and say, "Listen, here's what you need to do." If my cat started talking, I'd probably be more mesmerized by his voice than by what he was saying.

The best way to inspire someone is to actually take action. Talk and planning can happen for months and years, but action is immediate and demonstrative. Since animals don't speak our language per se, their lessons are in their actions.

This book has taken me on an incredible journey of self-discovery. I thought I would write these stories, publish them, and be done. That's not how it's worked. It's taken a lot longer than expected, and life has presented some challenges. Ironically, life has not gotten in the way but added depth and clarity to these lessons. I never expected writing a book to take me where I've been, and I wouldn't trade it for anything.

I hope that you find inspiration in these stories to make positive changes in your life. I also hope that you'll take some extra time with your animal friends to connect and show them some love.

Thank you,

Philip

See Things As They Are

Stalking like a secret spy, Amanda dashed behind the chair. She peeked around the corner and made another split-second dash to the bookcase. Eyes large as quarters, she peered and saw the target. One more leap and she'd complete her mission. Around the bookcase she peered, a few quick bounds, and then *slam*! She launched herself right into the sliding-glass door and let out a blood-curdling caterwaul.

Poor Puff! He was outside relaxing on the patio when Amanda decided to scare the bejesus out of him.

Like two siblings who didn't get along, Puff and Amanda were two of my cats. Puff was a gray, long-haired Persian cat who had beautiful fur that gave him a regal appearance. As a kitten he looked like a puff of fur—hence the name. He loved to bask in the sun, chase crumpled pieces of paper, and nap on the bed. His fur was so long that when he curled up on the bed, it was hard to distinguish his head from his tail.

He was a very gentle and loving cat that everyone thought was so beautiful. Every beauty has a beast, however, and his manifested when a brush or comb appeared. The other cats sat and purred while being brushed; not him. Comb his hair once and he'd give a low warning growl. Make another pass and the growl got louder. The next attempt you were bleeding, guaranteed. The groomer finally gave up, saying it was too stressful. Not for Puff, but for him!!

I adopted Amanda, from a no-kill shelter, so the other younger cat, Edmund, would have someone his own age to play with. It's always fun to be at grandma's house, but there's nothing like playing with friends your own age. A two-year-old Maine coon mix with striking brown eyes and thick brown fur, Amanda loved to chase balls and toy mice, and she challenged Edmund every chance she could.

She was intent on being queen of the house, so she challenged the others. It didn't take long for the Pavlovian effect to kick in, and the mere sight of Amanda would elicit hissing and tiptoeing in the opposite direction. I knew whenever I heard hissing, Amanda was up to her tricks again.

Today's altercation was a bit different than normal. Puff was stretched out on the patio enjoying a beautiful fall day. The air was crisp and the sun was warm, a perfect day to nap on the patio.

Perfect, that is, until Amanda launched herself into the door and scared him. He immediately ruffled his fur and began hissing. Never mind that he was safely on the other side of the glass. He immediately thought he was in trouble, and for good reason. Past experience showed that when she was near, there was going to be a smack down.

It was sad to see his relaxing day ruined for no good reason. He was safely on the other side of the glass. I thought if I showed him he was safe, he'd calm down. So I stood between him and the door, blocking her, to show him he was safe. It was too late; he continued to hiss and his stress level rose. His spa time had not gone well. The only solution was to move Amanda away from the door to restore some semblance of peace.

If you own cats, you'll recognize this as normal cat behavior. So what can we learn here?

See the situation for what it really is:

Puff was afraid of imminent attack because he could see Amanda right in front of him. Yet Puff was totally safe and didn't realize it. If he would've stopped and thought for a minute, he would've recognized that they were separated by a glass door. He knew from past experience that if she were going to attack, it would happen quickly.

Take a minute and think back to a stressful situation. How would it have been different if you had looked around at the surroundings and your place in them? Was there a "glass door" that was keeping you "safe" but you didn't see it? Were things really as you initially saw them? From my experience, it's far too easy to assume that what we see is the truth, when actually the reality is very different.

For example, I sent a friend a message one day that required a response. I didn't hear back at all, and I was a little miffed. If I send you a message, I expect to receive some sort of response—yes, no, maybe. My friend responded the *next day*, and I already had that "whatever" attitude. In reality, my message wasn't received till the next day. My friend had responded as soon as *he* saw it. Technology!!!

It's funny how quickly I assumed that my friend was ignoring me and became upset about it. I had expected a prompt response and when I didn't receive it, copped an attitude. In reality, it was nothing more than a technical glitch. 'Course I could've just called, but that would've been too easy.

How many times do we take something seemingly insignificant and make it a huge problem? The larger we make the problem, the more stress we have. Why do we have to make it larger anyway? Don't we have enough to do?

Next time a stressful situation comes your way, take a minute and analyze the whole picture. Step back and see the situation for what it is.

Respond the way we want to be treated:

Did you notice Puff's response to Amanda? He returned her aggression with his aggression. That just escalated the process. He could've just walked away. Even though they were separated by glass, they still managed to antagonize each other with their responses. Sound familiar? How many times have we made unpolite gestures from our car windows?

When in a tense situation, your reaction has a key impact on how the situation plays out. When Puff saw Amanda hissing, he could've ignored her or just went to another part of the patio. That would've nullified the whole situation. She may have continued her antics, but at least he would have been in peace. I'm sure if he ignored her long enough, she would've left. People are the same way. It's hard to argue with someone who won't respond.

How often do we respond in kind versus diffusing the situation? Ever respond rudely to someone who is rude? You may think you're justified by giving them their own medicine, or it may feel good for a bit because "you showed them." Realistically, you're just making the situation worse. If you don't like rude people, why on earth be one?

Besides, you don't know what that person is going through at the time. How good is your attitude when you have a raging headache or you've just received unpleasant news? Personally, when life is tough, I'm not the kindest or most exciting person to have around.

Flip the situation around: how does it feel when you have a down day and people treat you rudely? Doesn't make you feel any better, does it? Yet when someone is unexpectedly kind, it just makes your day. The whole day could be going south, and a few kind words totally change the day.

Looking back, how would your stressful situations have been different if you had responded differently? You don't have to sacrifice yourself or your values, but you can let some things go. There is nothing wrong with not responding or to respond in a way that diffuses the situation. Just consider how you'd like to be treated in that situation.

Often our habit is to respond defensively. This often escalates the situation—which brings us to the final point.

Respond from conscious thought instead of reacting out of habit:

Puff's response to Amanda was automatic and instant. After numerous encounters, he knew the ugly outcome of seeing and hearing her. A disclaimer: I kept them separated as much as possible, but there were times she just would flip out on him.

Now think about how you react to the situations you encounter; most often it's an automatic reaction.

Thanks to our years of conditioning and experiences, we have instance reaction for every situation; if this event happens, then react this way. Very little thought is required; our reactions just occur.

What happens when someone cuts you off in traffic? Is rude to you in line? Unfairly accuses you? If you're like me, you instantly have a defensive or retaliatory response. For me, driving is one of those hobbies where automatic reactions happen quickly.

I've had times where I find myself driving nicely and then a trigger will occur and instantly, I begin driving spiritedly. From not a care in the world, to an agenda in 10 seconds! The speed increases, I zip in and out of traffic gaps. I do enjoy driving and I must admit driving with ambition is quite fun!! But then then I'll ask myself; just what am I doing? I'm on my way to work, this isn't a race track. That split second breaks the routine, and I realize I should slow down. What's funny is I didn't consciously say, "I'm going to drive crazy through traffic." It just happened.

Not all of our automatic responses are a result of negativity. How about when someone compliments us? Extends praise for a job well done? Do we say a sincere thank you or just brush it off? I know I'll just sweep it aside and say "it was nothing" or "I bought this on sale." If we'd pause and fully accept the compliment, we'd see some positive benefits. We'd become more positive, more confident, and our attitude would definitely improve. Once you start looking, you begin to see just how much of our reactions are automatic.

We can change those automatic responses and improve our situations. Here's an example that wasn't easy to do but worked well. A co-worker drove me absolutely crazy because of his complete lack of motivation in solving a critical problem. After literally an hour plus of me clearly explaining how this was his responsibility, he still was adamant that it wasn't his problem. I'd spent all this time doing his work instead of my own, and his pay grade was significantly above mine!

My neck was tensing up and my attitude degrading by the second. An "automatic response" was about to come out—I was going to tell him in explicit language just what the problem was. It was not going to be a technical explanation, and it was definitely not going to be PG-rated.

I took a short walk to compose myself and find a resolution. I wasn't just going to walk away; there had to be a solution. Upon my return, I emailed my boss and his boss with a history of the problem, some polite suggestions for further action, and an offer to continue to help. The bosses realized the problem, and responded promptly, and the co-worker did what needed to be done.

My first response was to emphatically tell my co-worker he was lazy and incompetent. It would've felt really, really good but would have ruined my credibility and any hope of us working together. Once I stepped back, I found a better solution that worked well for all involved.

Changing from reaction out of habit to responding out of conscious thought is not easy. I can tell you from firsthand experience. I still react and spew things that I wish I didn't. It's a work in progress that's for sure.

I could tell you to just stay calm and focus, which does work. However, when someone is in your space, unloading on you, it's unbelievably hard to not react. If you corner any animal, they'll fight back and we aren't that different.

The best way I've found is to focus on myself. I know it sounds selfish and I've been called that before. But you have to take care of your health and well-being, no questions asked. Stiff necks, tight shoulders, headaches, and upset stomachs are not good for anyone. Reacting to situations and being stressed is just bringing on more of those physical ailments.

Responding out of conscious thought will mitigate the stress because you're responding in a manner that is good for all involved. Although I must confess, I have my days when I'm pretty sure grabbing a baseball bat would be the best solution.

Whenever a situation arises and you instantly feel like reacting, take a few seconds and interrupt that pattern. Think about how you'd like to be responded to, think about what's best at this time, think about what will be the most positive effect on your health and then respond from a conscious thought.

In conclusion, the next time you're feeling stressed or anxious, or facing a problem, take a minute, take ten minutes, or take a walk if possible. See the situation for what it really is and is not. It's easy to make assumptions and trump up a small issue into a massive problem.

And finally, the challenging one. Respond from conscious thought instead of reacting from ingrained habit. It's not easy, but once you start, you'll find your world changing for the better. You'll be in more control of your emotions instead of them controlling you.

Implementing these principles will not stop every stressful situation, but at least we won't be creating any more unnecessarily.

Just Keep Digging

What a beautiful turtle! Unlike the wild gopher tortoises that are a dirty gray and often covered in dirt, this little guy was clean and shiny. His eyes were bright, his neck was a light tan, and his bronze shell appeared to have been waxed or oiled—obviously someone's pet. He was under my parked car, so I figured he had escaped. I told all my neighbors about my find and waited for the normal "lost pet" signs to appear. Days and weeks went by, and no one missed their turtle.

A quick online search showed he was an African Sulcata. One quote said, "Eats like a cow, poops like a cow." The story began to unfold: this little plate-sized turtle was destined to weigh 100–150 pounds and live about that many years. Talk about a lifelong pet!

No one claimed him and I couldn't just turn him loose, so I named him Ben. From day one he displayed such a happy personality. His mouth curled up naturally on the sides so that he always appeared to be smiling. He didn't bark, meow, bay, or make any other noise. He was totally silent. All you'd hear were his steps through the foliage.

Everyone thought he was so cute, and the main question was, "What does he eat?" A little bit of everything! Grass, bright-pink hibiscus flowers, yellow flowers, bananas, grapes, strawberries, and anything colorful he would chomp on. Ladies with red toenails soon had him nibbling on their toes. I even saw him try to eat a green sleeping bag. He must've thought it was the largest green bean on the planet!!

Turtles normally live in burrows, but I didn't have one so he lived on the patio. The patio was large, fenced-in, and complete with flowers, plenty of dirt, and places to explore. A couple of palm trees graced the entrance, a jasmine bush scented the night air, and an herb garden and other greenery resided in this perimeter area. You could frequently find Ben walking through his little forest foraging.

For turtle enrichment, I'd let him out into the common area. The common area was a large grassy spot that was well manicured. He loved that and walked around for hours and ate grass, flowers, or other plants. I sometimes thought he was more sheep than turtle. When the grass was really tall, he'd leave a random trail of smashed grass—not quite crop circles, but the neighbors always wondered what made such markings in the lawn.

Ben didn't like to be brought in after his excursions, so like the cats, he figured out how to hide. Turtles are supposed to be slow, but I could turn away for just a couple of seconds and he'd be gone. Literally, he'd be there one minute and gone the next. I'd usually find him under a bush or a tree.

Ben loved that common area, but I was gone most of the day, which meant he was stuck on the patio. I'd come home from work and be greeted by his little head poked out under the gate looking at the grass. You could see the frustration on his little wrinkled face. "The entire yard is just a few feet away, but this darn gate is keeping me here."

When you really want something, you'll figure out a way to get it—and Ben was no exception. One day I found a small hole in the dirt near the gate. A few days later, the hole was bigger, and it continued to grow. My first thought was that the cats were up to something; but cats don't just dig holes.

Then one weekend, I found Ben in the hole excavating. He flicked his flippers and flung small amounts of dirt all over. It was hard to tell how much dirt left the hole and how much just ended up on his shell. It was interesting to watch him; I felt like I was watching a nature documentary firsthand.

The hole grew deeper and looked like a perfect turtle burrow. Good! I was glad to see him make his own natural place. Living in the shed was not turtle-like at all.

I was wrong! During one of his forays into the house, he must've seen a special on Alcatraz, because the burrow turned out to be an escape hole. For a little turtle, it was quite a feat of engineering. The hole was located in the perfect spot. He couldn't see the roots and obstructions on the other side of the fence, but he missed them all. When the hole was complete, he had an open run to the grass.

It was fun to watch him dig, and I didn't have the heart to stop him. He had worked so long and hard digging. I would've loved to have been there to see him emerge victorious, but his final escape occurred during working hours. Can you imagine what he thought as he flung that last scoop of dirt, slid under the fence, and emerged on the other side free to eat all the grass he liked and go wherever he wanted? What a feeling!!!

I was happy he was no longer a captive pet, but also sad because I missed the little guy. Where did his adventures take him? Was he in the woods, under a bush, in someone's patio? As I pondered those thoughts, here came a familiar sight. Ben walked down the sidewalk, like nothing unusual was going on, through the open gate, and right into the shed.

I stared in disbelief. He dug himself out, wandered among the townhomes (they all look alike), and returned home in the evening. Considering pizza delivery guys with GPS get lost in there, that's pretty impressive.

So now I had a dilemma: did I close the hole and keep him safe or leave it open and let him roam around the neighborhood? I was concerned that he would be run over, someone else would keep him, or worse, someone would use him for turtle soup. Believe it or not, I did have a few friends tell me how they'd cook him.

I considered it all and came to the conclusion that if he were in the wild, he'd encounter similar dangers. I left the hole open so he could enjoy his freedom of choice. He could sleep in the shed all day or go explore the yard.

As the weeks went on, my neighbors told me the places they'd seen him during the day. Based on their reports, he definitely made the rounds. One lady even said that he went inside her house and wandered around her living room. When in our home, he'd take a poop in the corner. All I could think of was him taking a healthy poop in her living room! Thankfully, she never mentioned that.

He continued to come and go at will. For safety, we put a mailing-label sticker on his shell so that people knew where he belonged. Usually around 6 p.m. he'd walk through the gate and into the shed. When the gate was closed, he'd come back in through his hole. It always amazed me that he knew where to return after walking all over the neighborhood.

Every time I tell this story, people are impressed that he always came home. Usually animals leave and don't come back. I think there are very important lessons we can glean from Ben's adventure.

Visualize your dream:

Every day, Ben looked under the gate and saw his dream. He could see the green blades of grass and smell the wonderful scent after it was freshly cut. Rabbits and gopher tortoises wandered by and possibly said hello. Everything he wanted was right there, and he could see it, smell it, and almost taste it. In addition, when I let him out, he could experience the dream firsthand. He felt the grass on his flippers, tasted the different varieties of grass and weeds. He could walk wherever he wanted and never set foot on concrete. I'm sure those memories flooded back each time he peered under the gate. Every day, he probably said, "Someday I'm getting out of here." He had a clear vision of his dream.

I did something similar when I wanted a new car. I browsed pictures, read reviews, looked up any and every specification, and of course compared prices. It was fun to do the research, but there wasn't that sensory connection. What really motivated me though were the test drive, the spacious interior, the cool displays and controls, and the smooth, powerful acceleration. The test drive was where I experienced what I really wanted. The final experience that put me over the top was the twenty-four-hour rental. That's where I put MY stuff in the trunk and drove around like it was mine. Shortly after, I found exactly what I wanted and purchased it.

Visualizing your dreams isn't just about physical things. It can be used for anything you want to achieve. See it in your mind before you achieve it.

Take a look at the dreams you have lined up. Are some of them stagnant? Have you seen them already realized in your mind? If not, take the time to visualize the dream already received. One of the best ways to get motivated is to experience your dream firsthand.

Test-drive a new car, visit an open house, try on new clothes, talk with a friend who just received a promotion. If you're dreaming of something less tangible, then talk to people who are living what you want, and feel the energy and excitement.

Whether you're just starting to list dreams or some are sitting stagnant, get your dream off paper and into your senses, and watch your motivation level skyrocket.

Prepare for the unexpected:

If you've ever dug a hole for a fence post, a well, or anything else, you know there are plenty of challenges waiting above and below the surface. Ben's excavation was no different. He dug in the rainy season so often that the hole would become a swimming pool. He'd have to wait days till the ground dried in order to dig again. Ironically, he was really good at predicting the weather. When he wouldn't come out of the shed, we knew it was going to rain.

When the ground was dry, the cats loved the fresh dirt Ben dug up. The cats regularly dug in Ben's hole, but it wasn't to help him. They would take a stinky poop in his hole and then cover it back up. Just imagine: you're excited about working on your dream, and midway you find that someone took a crap right in the middle of it. Now you have to deal with this stinky mess before you can go on. Darn cats!!! That explains why Ben would deliberately walk over to the cats and nip at their tails.

Those were just a couple of the obstacles for Ben's adventure. Yet he continued on. If the hole was wet, he went on with his regular day of eating and sleeping. If he found crap, he'd dig around it and continue on with his work. I'm not sure he had a plan for all the obstacles he might encounter, but he did keep making progress in spite of them.

What are your goals that are stagnant or haven't been started yet? Are you like myself and a lot of people who are afraid of all the unknowns? Are you afraid of finding a pile of crap midway through? We all know we are bound to find a pile of crap somewhere. It's the pile of crap, the pool of water, what's in the water, and other things that paralyze us.

Personally, I have a hard time getting moving because I like to know everything from start to finish. Of course, this is almost impossible, so I have to figure it out as I go. After numerous classes and seminars, I've learned that the best way to handle the unknowns is to plan for them up front.

For example, if you're changing careers, plan for being unemployed for an extended period. What would you do? How would you pay your bills, find another position, get by, etc.? Get that all out on paper, before you even start.

What if you didn't like the new career? What if your new boss or co-workers drove you crazy? What if your dream job required relocation? You can look at all of these and become very fearful, but that is not the idea. The idea is to realistically plan for these worst-case scenarios before you start. Once you have a plan for your worst-case scenarios, you can confidently move forward because you know what to do.

You've probably already planned for the best case, so by planning for the worst case(s), you've eliminated that "what if" fear. Sure there are risks involved, but you're much better prepared this way.

Even with a good plan, not everything will be perfect, and sometimes you'll have to be creative to get things done. In the end, that is what will make the success more valuable.

Take action:

Ben knew what the grass felt like and tasted like, and he knew the joy of being free. That was enough motivation for him to take action. The first thing he tried was to sit by the gate and "run" out each time I opened it. A turtle can move faster than you expect when it wants something.

One memorable time, I opened the gate and he went for the escape. Just as I was getting ready to lean down to bring him in, two cats ran right over the top of him on their way out. As I dodged out of the way, I thought, "What is this, a jailbreak?" Animals: they stick together.

Sometimes he'd "protest" and sit in front of the gate so I couldn't open it. That wasn't a problem when I was *inside* the patio. When I was outside and wanted to come in, it became difficult. I'd push on the gate and he'd just climb into his shell, which made it almost impossible to move him. It was like there was a big rock on the other side of the door. I'd have to firmly push on the gate and slide him out of the way. He'd hiss and grunt about it, but he wasn't about to get up and move.

Now that he knew he could get out periodically, his next step was to keep from being brought back inside. That's when he adopted a tactic the cats use: hide. Instead of walking in the open grass, Ben would spend his time under the bushes. Each townhome had bushes that bordered the fence and other areas of the building, so there were a lot of places for him to hide. Sometimes it'd take me half an hour just to find him!! What does every good parent do? Right—I'd either only let him out supervised or not let him out at all.

These actions let me know what he wanted, but to achieve his goal, he really needed something different. That's when he began to dig the hole. Even though digging a hole was second nature to Ben, there were a lot of unknowns. He didn't know how deep he'd have to dig to get under the fence. He didn't know if there was a root system or other barrier that would prevent him from his escape.

I or someone else could've filled the hole in just when he was close to being finished. Those are pretty serious considerations when you're digging with only your flippers. It's not like taking a shovel and finishing in fifteen minutes. This was a several-week process for him.

Ben took action toward his goal, but he didn't do just one thing and quit. He kept trying methods till he found one that worked. Each method he tried required more effort, but he kept moving forward till he achieved it.

Think about the goals you've achieved and the amount of action it took. Personally, some of my goals required me to reach much deeper than I expected.

Now think about goals that you aren't making progress toward or haven't even started. Have you taken action which didn't work as planned and then given up? What would happen if you looked at what didn't work, changed it, and tried again? It took Ben three tries to escape the patio, and it didn't happen overnight.

What would happen if you just took action, any action? If you did, you would accomplish two things: (1) you would've taken action, and (2) you would know what works and what doesn't. Just one simple step will answer two questions. Seems silly we all don't take more action, doesn't it?

Ben was able to see his dream every day and which kept him focused. Despite the unexpected obstacles, he continued to take action, making corrections as necessary. Whatever goal you have, get it into your senses every day through visualization or firsthand experience. As you plan, plan for failure so you can ensure success. You may have to adjust course or even get some crap on you, but keep digging—you'll get it done.

Climb That Fence and Take That Leap

"Your cat is on the fence again." Of course he's on the fence: I'm not dressed to go outside. The probability of him being on the fence and escaping is in direct proportion to my attire. He can sit on the patio calmly for hours, but as soon as I change clothes, he's gone. It's like he knows when he can best escape from home.

Such is life with Edmund, our seventeen-pound Siamese that is all attitude—or should I say cat-itude. Even though he can push my buttons, he and I are very much alike. We love to explore, enjoy a long nap in the sun, eat good food, and do anything outdoors day or night.

Edmund is named in honor of Sir Edmund Hillary and has lived up to his namesake by being the consummate explorer. Whether it's stalking under the bushes outside or spreading the contents of a grocery bag all over the floor, he has to check everything out.

With exploration in his blood, you can imagine that he doesn't stay on the patio for long. You'd think I'd know this, but I still have this "belief" that he'll just hang out on the chairs or under the plants. He continues to prove me wrong, and some days he is just like a little kid.

He'll sneak around and pretend he's just hanging out. Then I'll catch him making his way toward the fence and he'll shoot me one of those "can't stop me looks." The game is afoot! As I make my way toward him, he runs up the fence and then looks down as if to say, "I won."

Anyway, climbing the fence isn't the big deal; it's his exit from the top that is always intriguing. You see, the six-foot wooden fence is bordered by three-foot hedges all the way around. These aren't your pretty, soft hedges. These are leafy and prickly, and any encounter with them leaves significant reminders. I've had to deal with them while repairing sections of the fence, and I always end up bleeding or with lots of red marks.

Edmund could just leap off the top of the fence and hope for the best. That'd probably work, but that would be quite a leap. Edmund has a different take on it all. He leans over the outside of the fence, slides down face-first, and at the last possible second, catapults horizontally over the hedges.

He's done this for years, and I've yet to see him miss. The fact that he never misses is impressive because the hedges are always growing or being cut—so every escape is a different set of variables. Of course, he can't miss. If he misses, he'll impale himself, lose an eye, or in some other way severely wound himself.

Put yourself in his paws for a second. You need to escape from a second-story balcony, and the only way is to slide down the wall. Midway up this wall is a chain link fence with barbwire at the top to keep people out. Face first, you lean over and then let go. Faster and faster you descend as gravity takes full control. The barbed wire of the fence is coming closer and closer. This is going to hurt!!

At the perfect moment, you summon all of your strength, push yourself horizontally off the wall, and clear the fence. Whew! You missed the barbed-wire fence, but you're still in the air and have to nail the landing. Edmund makes these escapes look easy, but I'm sure I'd end up in the bushes or face down on the sidewalk.

For the longest time, his escaping was just another one of those "Edmund annoyances." Then one day I started looking at all the details and made some interesting observations.

He and I are a lot alike:

So why does Edmund escape? Because he wants outside is the obvious answer, but it's deeper than that. He wants to be free to do what he wants. Occasionally, he'll visit the neighbors, but ironically, 99 percent of the time he escapes and sits under the car or the bushes.

I sit on the patio as well, but after a while, I'm out the gate and in the grass or somewhere close. I just like being outside and being free of fences, cubes, and any confinement. Unless I'm running or biking, I don't go far either. Just being outside of the fence is freeing.

When I walk down to the mailbox, Edmund is usually right with me or will blast off full speed across the parking lot. Like me, he enjoys a good walk or run.

When Edmund was younger, I tried very hard to keep him contained in the patio. It became a battle of wits to see who would win. Often I found my latest contraption bent, pulled down, or crawled under and him outside. For me it was annoying; for Edmund it was something to challenge him and keep him occupied.

Then one day I hit the right combination of pieces, and he couldn't get out. He tried numerous times and finally gave up. Success!! I could leave him on the patio without worrying about him escaping. I didn't have to constantly watch him.

A few days later I looked at him on the patio, and he had changed. His beautiful Siamese blue eyes were no longer bright. In fact they looked gray. His entire countenance was low, and he just lay there with his head down. Nothing interested him; he just lay there like in a prison cell.

I remembered how much he enjoyed going outside and then remembered how much I love going outside. Even at work, I walk outside for a few minutes regularly just to clear my head. I looked down at him and in those sad eyes, saw myself. I saw a person who just wanted to be free to do what he wanted, when he wanted. To be trusted and allowed to have fun, or simply put, to be allowed to be free.

I guess deep down, I had erected my own barriers to progress. That same day, I removed every barrier I had put up, and it felt really freeing. Edmund's countenance immediately changed as well. His Siamese blue eyes came to life, and he had spring in his step again. He'd chase leaves and lizards, and with every step exuded life. My Edmund was back! I told him that I'd prefer he stay in the fence, but that if he wanted to go explore, to be careful and not go far. That was several years ago, and the understanding is still working.

He still escapes, but he doesn't go far and always comes home. I make sure he has his collar on at all times as well. What is really funny is that some days, he escapes, and I'm just not in the mood for it. I'll angrily fling open the gate and find him sitting in the grass. I'd really like to yell at him, but then he looks at me with those gorgeous blue eyes and I decide to sit in the grass with him. I'll look up at the stars, gaze at the sunset, or just feel the grass within my toes. Within a few minutes, all my cares melt away, and I realize his escape wasn't just for him. It was just what I needed.

I don't advocate letting pets run free unsupervised, but pay attention to your pet's behavior and then your own. You may find that you both want the same thing and that sometimes their "antics" are a reminder of who you really are and just what you need.

He enjoys the journey:

When Edmund escapes, often he'll play hide-and-seek on the patio as I'm trying to round him up. Then he'll beeline to the top of the fence and meow as if to say, "Can't catch me!" He'll then patrol the top of the fence, making sure every inch of it is in order.

Lately, he's taken to sitting on the fence for a half hour or more, just enjoying the view. Whatever the method, he always takes time to enjoy the whole journey. Instead of immediately leaping off the top to freedom, he enjoys the view and the advantages it offers. It's never a stressful experience for him.

If it were me, I'd climb that fence and be on the other side as quick as possible and be gone. "View? What view? I didn't see anything—let's go!" Sound familiar? I am known for being focused on tasks at hand and placing fun on the back burner. "We can always have fun at the end; right now let's get this done."

It's easy to get caught up in the excitement of achievement and forget about everything else. I know people who have a lot of fun but really aren't moving forward in their lives. On the other hand, I know people who are very successful and work all the time and hardly see their family or have any fun. I've done that; don't need to do that again. The key is to find that often-elusive balance.

One way to have fun is to pause along the way and enjoy the experience. Sometimes Edmund will sit in the shadow box and look around at the plants inside the fence and observe the lizards. He hasn't given up on his goal of reaching the top; he's just pausing along the way.

A pause can be exactly what we need to see where we've come from and acknowledge progress. A pause can also be the perfect time to reevaluate the effectiveness of our actions. Take a day to kayak, go for a hike, or whatever you do for fun will be good for you and your progress. You'll feel rejuvenated and see things more clearly.

Another way to bring fun into the process is to change your routine. Instead of working out at the gym, go outside. Instead of researching at home, go to the library. Meet some friends and brainstorm. Change the usual routine and bring fun into it. We all know that we'd rather do something fun than something arduous.

For example, I love to write, but sitting in front of a PC on the weekend just isn't my cup of tea. The sun is shining, the sky is blue, and the world is waiting. Instead of putting off writing, I take my writing outdoors. Sometimes it's just the patio; other times it's the park. I'm having fun and working on my goals at the same time.

Having fun doesn't mean not making progress. It just means changing the process to something you actually enjoy. It will be different for everyone, so do what works for you and keeps you energized and moving.

Use what you have to its fullest:

Watching Edmund is always entertaining because he uses what he has to the fullest. He doesn't wait for someone to bring him a ladder or lay boards against the fence. He doesn't wait for his nails to grow longer, for the hedges to be trimmed, the fence to dry, or any other excuse. He uses whatever he has right here and right now to reach his goal.

He still is adapting to and learning about the ever-changing outdoor conditions. One day the wind blew a large palm frond into his face and practically knocked him off the fence. He regained his footing and cat composure in true cat style: "that wasn't me that almost fell off." Another time the hedges had grown much taller than usual, which meant a longer jump. Every time, no matter what, he used what he knew and adjusted accordingly.

This lesson was particularly valuable to me because I'm always thinking I "need" something to get a project or goal started. Consequently, I'll put it off because I think I don't have everything I need to get started. In reality, I already have most of what I need, or at least enough to get a solid start.

To alleviate this, I'll take a goal that I have in mind and list what I think it will take to make it happen. Then I'll list what I already have to make it happen. Surprise! I usually have a substantial part of the list already. Next, I list what I really need to do or acquire and move forward from there.

This has been very helpful in getting moving on some long-standing projects. Often goals seem out of reach because "I don't have this." In reality, you may still need "this or that," but you also already have "all of this!!" If you'd use what you have right here and right now, you could make substantial progress. Once you get started, you have momentum and it's easier to keep moving. Just getting started is usually the hardest part.

Whatever you want to accomplish, take a look at what you already have that you can use today and you'll be surprised at how quickly you can get started. Once you know what you have, you can exploit that to its fullest potential.

Going it on your own can be the hard way:

Edmund meows to me and often sits by the gate wanting outside. I don't let him out for a variety of reasons: The lawn guys are out there, there are people outside with their dogs, or it could rain at any minute. He'll follow me meowing or will wait for some sign that I'm going to let him out. If he doesn't see it, he'll take matters into his own hands and climb out. Once outside, he immediately knows why I didn't let him out.

If he would just wait for me, I'd open the gate at the right time. He wants what he wants right now, so he takes the hard way. I admire his sheer determination and ability to make things happen.

However, I can't help but think that if he'd wait for me, he could just walk out the gate. Simple and easy—no chance of falling in the bushes, pulling a nail while climbing, or falling off the top of the fence.

Yet I totally understand him because I'm the same way. I want what I want right now. I may wait for a bit, but then I'm off to go get it. Once the "If you want something done right, do it yourself" mentality kicks in, I'm gone.

There have been plenty of times I've attempted to bully my way through situations and then finally gave up. Then, when I least expected it, the proverbial door was opened for me or a different situation worked out easily. We may think we know the best way to have what we want and the best time. Often we overlook that help from something beyond us that knows what's best. Everyone has their own name for it, but I'll simply call it a higher power. Knowing what's best for us, this higher power can bring us substantial help and relief from our stress.

Edmund doesn't know why I won't open the gate for him. Yet I know that what is on the other side isn't good for him at that time.

If you're always climbing fences instead of walking through gates, stop and ask for help from a higher power. Why make it hard on yourself? When you ask for help, also ask for the clarity to recognize the help and the courage to act on it. It is possible that your request has been answered but you've been too busy to see it.

I enjoy the fun of climbing fences and conquering obstacles, but I know there is often an easier way. So ask for help—maybe a gate or door will be opened for you. Climbing maybe just what you need. Just try not to climb the fence when the gate is already wide open…

Whatever goals you're taking on, whether by choice or by life situations, make sure to enjoy the journey. It's not always easy, but look for the good in all situations. Take the time to pause and have some fun along the way. Chances are you won't be this way again, so be sure to capture the memories. While you're at it, use everything you have to its fullest. Don't wait for someone or something. You probably have enough to get started and figure out the rest. And finally, ask for help along the way. It could make the journey significantly easier, and you'll learn what you need to the first time.

So be like Edmund, and Climb That Fence and Take That Leap!!

Whatever It Takes to Make It

Careful, don't step in the poop! I gingerly walked around the small pile in the sand. As I walked past, I noticed there was something unusual. Not that I'm a poop expert, but raised on a farm and a pet owner, I've seen my share of poop.

Upon closer inspection, it wasn't poop at all, but baby sea turtle hatchlings! Their eyes closed and baking in the direct midmorning sun, I thought they were dead. I gently moved the sand around them, and they started moving! Sea turtles making their trek to the ocean is one of those things you have to see. Today was my lucky day and theirs too…

It was 10 a.m. on a sweltering, hot summer Florida morning. Just being in the sun was hot, and attempting to walk barefoot on the sand was a burning experience. I was wearing shoes, and my feet were hot. I could only imagine these little babies baking in the sand.

At the top of the stack, the top turtle was draped over another one, like they'd been out drinking the night before and just passed out here. He began to move slowly and then tentatively looked around, just like I do after an afternoon nap. You know, that groggy, slow-moving feeling.

He flapped his tiny flippers enough to move off the other turtle and looked straight up at me for a few long seconds. I wasn't sure if he looked at me in wonderment or if he was trying to communicate. It was one of those moments I won't forget. He made a quick circle in the sand around the other heads poking out. He stopped by the one he had been resting on, tapped it on its head with his flippers as if to say "wake up, it's time to go!" and then headed toward the ocean.

From the turtles' point of view, the ocean was at least two hundred feet. This isn't much for a human, but for something the size of a quarter, that's a long trek. The little guy headed directly for the ocean without any deviation. Just straight for it. I don't know if he heard it or how else he knew where to go, but he just went. His little flippers were going double time as he went through the peaks and valleys of the sand.

The House of Refuge beach, located on the Treasure Coast, is surprisingly rocky. The rocky areas stretch for most of the beach and have millions of sharp little spires on them that make walking barefoot on them painful. Open-toe sandals and flip-flops are little consolation. At low tide, these rocky outcroppings can be five to six feet off the ocean floor.

There are places, though, where there is smooth beach between the rocks, and that is how the momma turtle made it this high on the beach to lay her eggs. Having made the trek up, she knew how to navigate back. However, this was the first time for the babies, who only knew one thing: water!!

This first little guy encountered the rock outcropping and had to have wondered, "What is this?" As he fumbled his way around, he ended up upside down a few times and had to scale "tall" ledges to get to the top. Imagine climbing flights of stairs with only your hands—no feet, no toes, just your hands!

Once on top, he didn't falter but just kept moving forward with amazing determination. He bobbled, rolled over, stumbled some more. As he neared the edge and the precipice that dropped five feet to the sand, he just kept moving full speed.

If you've had a pet turtle or watched them for any time, you know that turtles are very conscious of height and drop offs. I had a pet African Sulcata that would take five minutes to make the three-inch drop from the kitchen to the patio. He double- and quadruple-checked the height and the path.

Not so for this little, determined sea turtle. The order of the day was to keep moving and to move fast. He came to a ledge and fell down about one quarter of the way, landing on another ledge. His next wriggling motion launched him off a four-foot-high ledge right into the sand, upside down. You know turtles don't do well upside down. I walked down to look at him, and he was just wriggling and writhing trying to get righted. He finally stopped moving and just lay there...I watched him for a bit and he just lay there.

The hot sun, the long trek, and no water had sapped his energy. Now he lay upside down, within feet of the ocean waves. Even if it wasn't an endangered species, I couldn't just watch it lay there! Yet I know that I can't imprint it with human scent either. So I found a stick and gently rolled the little guy back on his feet.

Zoom!! He was off like a madman, again! They must serve some pretty strong espresso in that sea turtle nest!! The ocean is within sight; he's made it through the hot sand, off the tall rocky ledge, and just has a few feet to go.

Plop!! He fell into a deep human footprint. The soft, wet sand had held the large, deep shape perfectly. Moving his flippers nonstop and moving back and forth, he finally scaled his way out of the vertical walls of the footprint, only to fall into the next one. More wriggling, flippers flapping, and he's out just in time to catch the next wave. Which pushed him BACK onto the beach!!! Ugghhhh, so close.

The cool water was exactly what he needed for his second wind. He's gone back for round two. Fortunately, this wave has enough water to pull him into the ocean. At this point he can swim, and he is off on his amazing journey. Whew!! That's just to get to the beach, now he has to deal with rogue fishing line, birds, predation, trash, and whatever else the ocean and man toss at him.

By this time the rest of the hatchlings have begun their endeavor and look out—fifteen to twenty baby sea turtles making a mad dash for the water has made the normally quiet sand become alive. No two turtles take the same route. It looks like a scene from a horror movie with all these little black creatures crawling out of the sand and then going everywhere.

Following the general direction of the first turtle, they head straight for the rocks. The early daredevils scrambled up, around, and over the rocky area and flop off the five-foot high rock into the sand. Their speed and sheer volume made it appear that a conveyor belt is unloading hatchlings. One after another, flop, flop, and without missing a beat, they headed for the water. Like the pioneer hatchling, some landed upside down but manage to right themselves.

It is said that only one in a thousand sea turtle hatchlings make it to adulthood, and this journey demonstrates how that occurs. While many hatchlings have made it to the water, numerous hatchlings have become stranded on the rocks. They can't find their way off, and the 95-degree midday sun is rapidly draining their energy.

I'm hot and sweaty just watching. They flit around the rock spires, searching, landing upside down and rolling back into the sand, desperately trying to find the sea. Some are just sitting still on the rocks, thoroughly exhausted.

The rock formations also have periodic holes that are about knee deep. In their excited fervor, a few of these hatchlings tumble into these holes. With no way to escape, these hatchlings are certain to die.

It is against the law, with hefty fines, to harass or bother sea turtles in any way, but I couldn't just let them die. Sure, survival of the fittest came to mind, but so did all of man's follies that brought this species to endangered status.

 Again, I used my small stick and would gently roll the hatchlings into my hat and then carry them down to the level portion of the beach where they could finish their trek to the sea. Crawling to the sea is part of their journey and their destiny.

I worked discreetly so as not to attract lots of people and successfully helped all the stranded hatchlings make it to the ocean. What a great feeling!! A species endangered by man gets a chance because of man. I thought it was a fair trade…

Watching and helping these little hatchlings was an unforgettable experience. As I watched and re-watched my videos and related stories, I began to see some important lessons I could apply to my life.

Clearly defined goals:

These guys know their goal: get to the ocean no matter what. They have never seen the ocean or even this particular beach, but their goal is crystal clear. They don't know the obstacles they'll encounter on the ground or from above, but they just go for it. They figure it out as they go.

Think about any of your accomplishments, and what is the common thread? A well-defined goal. Whether it was passing a test, losing ten pounds, running a half marathon, or changing careers, you knew the end result and worked toward it.

Unlike the hatchlings, you're familiar with your surroundings and have the luxury of researching and determining your goal. You don't have to know how you'll achieve it yet; you just need to know exactly what you want.

Now if the hatchlings were not clear on where to go, they'd never get to the ocean. There are too many distractions & obstacles. Like them, know where you're going. You don't have to know how; just know where.

What is it that you HAVE to do? What is it that you KNOW with absolute certainty?

Determination:

A sea turtle hatchling is tiny and can easily fit in the palm of your hand with room to spare. Yet these hatchlings must bust out of their eggs, which are laid underground, and climb up through the dirt to reach the surface. Then they must tackle the trek to the sea, which is the most difficult and dangerous part of their journey.

The sand is filled with numerous obstacles; footprints are like the Grand Canyon. The smallest trash can be deadly. One hatchling got tangled in a 2-foot piece of fishing line. It was only a matter of seconds before it was wrapped up in the line and immobile.

YES I removed it. Regardless of Darwin's theory of survival of the fittest, everyone gets their shot on my watch. What you do with your shot is up to you...

In this case, the hatchlings had to navigate the rocky ledges and then jump off. Now think about this: three-inch hatchlings make a leap from a sixty-inch-high rock. That's a long way for such a small animal, and it lands and keeps right on going. As I watched these hatchlings make their trek, I was blown away by their sheer determination. Falling in footprints, getting turned upside down on the rocks, and eventually falling over the cliff—nothing stopped them; they were constantly moving and searching for the path to the ocean. Their life literally depended on them reaching the ocean.

Back to you and me: are we anywhere close to that determined in anything we do? Just think of what we could do if we did *whatever* it took to reach our goal—if no matter the obstacle, we just climbed up and over, and even jumped off if needed. Whatever it took, no questions asked.

Now add this caveat: what if your life depended on it? Several friends have experienced this exact dilemma with their health: either change their diet and begin exercising or die early. Whenever you face an ultimatum like that, you find the courage to step up. What about finding that courage before it becomes life threatening? What about summoning that courage because your life (mental, spiritual, career, love, health, etc.) depends on it?

Realistically, it does: when you're unhappy, unfulfilled, distressed, depressed, etc., it's wearing you down. You have to be determined to make the changes YOU need to make. As I sit here and write, I'm the first one to tell you I'm a "do it later" person. When faced with ultimatums, I easily step up and do great things, but otherwise I don't expend that much effort. It's a little hard—oh well, maybe I'll find an easier way. Completing this book took a lot of determination for me. Sure, I loved writing it and sharing the stories, but it required a lot of typing and editing. When it's a beautiful day outside, the last thing I want to do is sit in front of a computer. You have to be determined to do whatever it takes.

A little help from above:

In spite of their dogged determination, many of the hatchlings found themselves in holes or completely spent and not near their goal. They tried as hard as they could, but they were at the end of their rope. Unable to escape from the holes in the rocks, they were sure to slowly die. Stuck on the rocks upside down, they'd bake in the 90-degree summer sun or become bird food. What about their clear goals? What about their determination? Was it all for nothing?

Not at all, because I "happened" to be there. I was enjoying the ocean and decided a video would be perfect to show friends. It was on that trip to the car, which just occurred to me out of the blue, that I saw these guys. If I had not had the "idea" to get my phone, I would've never seen them.

Thanks to my experience as a volunteer at various wildlife/animal rescue agencies, I knew exactly what to do. Gently, without human touch, I rescued the stranded ones and placed them on the beach with a clear shot to the water. For them, they received the help they needed just in time. Imagine if some kid with a stick came along and decided to poke them or just throw them in the ocean.

Note that I didn't just put them in the water; they still had to make that critical part of their journey. Imagine excitedly going along your journey and then expectantly falling into a hole. You look and look, but there is no way out. Looking up at the top of the hole, you realize you physically do not have the means to get out. One wrong turn, and your life, your dreams, your hopes, your future—done. Imagine feeling that and then being lifted out of the hole and given a second chance. Imagine how elated you'd feel, how thankful it'd be to have a second chance.

You are not alone in your journey. You may not see the help that is available, and it may not come as you expect it, but know that it is there. In my experiences, the help often comes unexpectedly and from a source so obscure that there is no doubt it's from above. Whomever or whatever you believe in, just know that help will be there when you need it.

Exploring Keeps Me Alive

I'll never forget the dinner invitation that day. "Please bring your favorite dessert; and take home a kitten." Our friend thought it'd be fun if we all adopted one of her kittens. All of her kittens would have a good home, and we'd all be related through the cat family. It was an ingenious solution.

The kittens climbed all over us, played with our shoestrings, and were just so cute. Most baby animals are cute, but there's something about a kitten; the innocence (which doesn't last long!), the playfulness, the bright eyes.

It's often said animals pick their owners, and now I know why. A quiet, small brown kitten with a bent tail came over and sat in my lap. It was so cute and cuddly, but there were other kittens to see. A short time later, this little one wandered over and climbed in my lap again.

That was eighteen years ago, and Keiko's favorite place was always my lap. Riding in the car, watching TV, sitting outside, or at the park—the lap was THE place to be.

Keiko grew into the most beautiful seal point Siamese cat-dark chocolate colors, deep blue eyes, and the famous Siamese kinked tail.

Keiko didn't puke on the carpet or swing from the curtains, but she did have her own set of quirks. One day I noticed my dress socks had a hole in them, so I tossed them. The next week, another pair had a hole in them. Everyone knows that dress socks get holes in them, but not every week.

This went on for weeks, and I could not find the cause. My toenails were cut, shoes were fine, even checked the washing machine. Where were these mysterious holes coming from? The landlord said it was probably our cat. Naw, that couldn't be. Guess what? We walked into the bedroom one afternoon and found Keiko sitting on the pile of laundry gnawing on a dress sock.

Mystery solved!!! Socks were just the beginning as she demonstrated a gourmet taste for laundry. T-shirts, socks, any clothing that felt really soft had Keiko's signature holes in it. I'd pick up a t-shirt and it'd be riddled with tiny holes. I don't remember why I just didn't put my laundry away.

Aside from eating soft material, one of Keiko's other favorite things was to ride in the car. I'd lower the window, and she'd lean out and put her head into the wind. Her eyes would close, her ears would blow, and I could see this sense of contentment just come over her. It was like she was born to fly. Other drivers always did a double take when they saw her, and then they'd laugh. You knew they went home and said, "You wouldn't believe what I just saw."

Since she loved riding in the car, she was brought along for weekend trips. I'd leave her in a hotel room, and she'd lounge on the bed watching TV. I'd return after a long day of exploring, and she'd look at me with one of two expressions: "Finally, you're back. Where is my dinner?" or "Back so soon?" I was *sooo* enjoying my nap."

If she was bored sitting on the bed, she'd soak up the sun in the window. Every time someone walked by, they'd comment on her. I wondered what she thought about all the different people walking by. Was she making up stories, as I often do?

She was a great buddy, and we went all kinds of places together: the beach, the park, road trips. She was with me through everything: divorce, cross-country moves, career changes, relationship changes, mood swings, personal growth, etc. She was there for the good, the bad, the ugly, and the unknown.

One day her breath smelled unbelievably nasty. It was putrid. Wow! What did she eat? I thought it was just her diet or that I didn't brush her teeth. The bad breath continued, and I eventually took her to the vet.

Imagine my dismay when I learned she had a form of mouth cancer called feline oral squamous cell carcinoma. It wasn't curable and was slowly eating away her jaw. It was like a strange alien life form that you'd see on a horror movie. I looked at the X-rays, and you could see where the jaw was physically missing. This was just the beginning. The cancer would continue to dissolve the jaw till she couldn't eat or drink.

I was devastated; how could this happen to such a wonderful cat? If she was mean, attacked everyone, or was just a pain in the butt, then I might see how this could happen. Keiko had never been anything but kind.

The questions and guilt raced through my mind. Did I do something wrong? I don't smoke or use tobacco. Should've given her purified water? Should've given her higher-quality food? Maybe there was something to those holistic diets? Even though the vet assured me there was nothing I did to cause it, I still felt to blame. OK, so I didn't cause it; could I have stopped it?

The disease was horrible to watch as her jaw was literally being eaten away week after week. Teeth would fall out, skin would come off. It was like she was being tortured. The vet checked her several times, and she wasn't in pain.

Since the side of her jaw was disintegrating, food and water would just fall out. It was like having a leaky hose.

The joy of eating and drinking became necessary evils and very messy affairs. She'd drink water and it'd run down her chin, down her chest. Once done drinking, she'd have this long, dangling drool. Her paws were constantly wet, her eyes were dirty, and her tongue just hung out. She went from looking like a well-groomed princess to looking like something you'd find in an alley that was just barely alive. If animal care ever swung by, I was sure I'd be arrested for animal abuse.

As the end drew near, I took her for car rides any chance I could. I'd let her wander in the grass and spend hours with her after work. Instead of "having" to write, clean, or complete the usual tasks, I spent time with her. Like sand you're trying to hold in your palms, time was slowly slipping away, and I couldn't stop it.

The guilt train had pulled into the station, and there wasn't a departure time. Life had gotten in the way, and I had always been busy doing something. All of the fun things we used to do had been special occasions rather than the norm.

As the years had gone, a couple of cats joined the family. They were younger and required more attention. Keiko just quietly sat on the sidelines hoping to get an occasional pet or some real attention. Sad to say, but she became a fixture around the house, rather than the best friend I had once done everything with.

I really felt bad about the time we had lost. I felt like a failure, like I'd messed up, again!!! Here was a great friend that I had neglected and taken for granted.

The guilt and this incurable disease were overwhelming. Any point of the day would find me angry, in tears, or just totally not there. I felt completely helpless and was lost. I'm a fixer—I make things better, and I couldn't do anything. Or so I thought.

I was contemplating the whole situation when I felt an "insight" from somewhere beyond me. It said that I couldn't change the past at all, but I could change right now. Any action, anything at all, would be welcome.

So I immediately began doing anything for her and sometimes just being there. These times resulted in the unforgettable lessons and the rest of the story below. Thank God I took action…

Never stop exploring:

One Saturday afternoon, the weather was just perfect: crystal-clear blue sky, a slight breeze, and low humidity. It was the perfect day to get out, so I grabbed Keiko and off we went to one of my favorite parks.

This park is right on the river and has long boardwalks into the water that are really pretty. She was wrapped in a towel and sitting in my arms on the rail. We watched boats of all shapes and sizes sail by in the blue-green water. A gentle breeze blew in our faces, and pelicans provided an aerial show. You couldn't ask for a nicer day.

She then squirmed and wanted down to explore on her own. OK, I put her down, and she took off! I had to walk briskly to catch up to her. She poked her head through the rails and looked down at the water. Then off she'd go again, as if she was on a mission.

Off the boardwalk and in the grass, she plowed through and wandered up, over, down, or through anything she could. She almost went in a drainage pipe, under the boardwalk, into the marsh; she was hard to keep up with. Where did all of this energy come from?

As I contemplated the dramatic change in Keiko, I was reminded of my own situation. Keiko's issues were incurable, but mine were not. I was at a loss about my life: I was not doing what I wanted to do, I was not the person I wanted to be, etc.

The questions had become overwhelming again: What had happened to my relationship? What had happened to me? Why had I given up? Why was I at this point in my life?

Then it hit me: For many years, Keiko just slept and ate. She loved hanging out in the closet or under the bathroom sink. I'd come home, and she'd come out eat and then go back in. I often complained, "You don't do anything."

Yet I never took her anywhere, I never let her out, and I didn't give her any opportunities. I thought she was just getting old, and she was, but not how I thought. She was dying inside of boredom. In reality, we both were and just didn't know it.

Even terminally ill and a bit weak, she was so excited to be outside; she had big bursts of energy. She was exploring, doing something new and different, and expanding her horizons. Maybe she sensed she was short on time so she was living it up. She had become the cat I'd remembered—one of energy and fun.

Watching her made me think hard about my life. I had no reason to be unhappy, but I was. My life was mundane and boring, and somewhere along the way I had gotten very lost. I couldn't quite place it, but I knew something was really missing. I wasn't happy, wasn't fulfilled, and felt just plain stuck.

Consequently, I woke up unhappy, went to work unhappy, and eventually became severely depressed. My girlfriend would ask if I wanted to do something, and I'd just say no. I'd stay home and work around the house all weekend. There was always so much to do here that "couldn't wait." I'd spend all weekend around the house and then complain about not getting anything done.

Actually, I'd complain about everything. I hated my job, where I lived, the people I was with, the money I made, etc. It was like a dark cloud that was always there. I'd hoped for a sunny day but never did anything to change the situation for the better. For whatever reason, I was just not myself, and I hated it.

After spending the afternoon with Keiko, I remembered that I used to be very alive. Every holiday, I was on a plane to somewhere different. Every weekend, off on some adventure. I volunteered at places, I took classes, and I was always up to something. Always very busy, but consistently learning and growing.

Then I decided to move out of state and stopped doing all my activities because I wasn't going to be "here." I stopped living in the moment, living right now. Anticipating the move, I stopped doing things, thinking, "I'm leaving—no sense in signing up." Yet I didn't work that hard on the move, and when things didn't pan out I became lost.

I had stopped exploring, traveling, volunteering, doing all the things that I loved. When I didn't move, I didn't return to my previous venue of exploring; I stayed stuck in that land of being in between—neither here, nor there; not anywhere.

I lost my sense of adventure. I got bored and thought I'd seen it all. I'd tell people about cool places to see around town, but I wouldn't go see them. I could tell you fun things to do, but I wouldn't do them.

I lost my motivation to explore, and any excuse was enough. Not enough money, don't feel like driving, we've done that before, I've seen that already, and the list went on. I became stuck in that box of get up, go to work, come home, work out, eat, go to bed, etc.

This went on literally for a few years, which is why I became depressed and unhappy. There were brief moments, like a vacation or an achievement at work, that I'd wake up, but then I'd return to the same old grind. It was like trying to remove your boot from the suction of thick mud. You pull and pull, but it doesn't come out. You focus so much on the boot in the mud, you don't realize that the land around you is dry and you don't need boots.

Just before Keiko's illness, I was separated from my girlfriend for a bit and I was really alive. I thought it was the end of the relationship, but in reality it was me stepping up and taking action in my life. It was me getting back to exploring. I didn't want to sit home alone, so I went off and did things: ran half marathons, visited familiar places, just walked around the neighborhood, whatever it took just to do something. I saw new things while doing the familiar, I did new things which expanded me, and I felt so alive.

I've heard it said that once you stop learning, you die. Yet I didn't see it in my own life till I spent that afternoon with Keiko. When I stopped exploring and growing, I began slowly dying. As more dying occurred, it soon became my way of life. It was a long, slow slide to the bottom.

Whatever your status in life—single, married, employed, looking for work, or retired, remember to keep exploring!! Keep learning; keep moving forward. Do those things that stimulate you, that excite you.

Don't pass up an opportunity because you may not be here or there. Take advantage of everything you can. Sometimes changes take a year or two, and you will have missed out on doing something you really wanted. Plan for the future, but live for today.

Keep exploring; keep that sense of fulfillment alive!

Things come alive with attention:

Ever since I took Keiko to the park that day and let her out every evening, she was wired. Every morning she was under foot, walking around the kitchen and living room. I'd be upstairs getting dressed and here would come this spindly, almost wobbly cat blasting up the stairs. At times, it was really annoying to hear the constant meowing, so I'd pick her up. "What is your problem?" I'd ask. I thought she might be in pain. As soon as I picked her up, all I heard was the familiar sound of contentment: purring.

What had changed with her? I had not given her any different medicine, and she had become skinnier by the day. But something was obviously different.

Let's see, she went from just hanging around the house and receiving whatever "leftover" attention I had to being the first to receive attention. She received my attention first and foremost, and we spent quality time together.

Even if I had other things I "should have" been doing, I took time to make sure she went outside and had fun. The more time I spent with her, the more alive she became.

Just like a plant that requires water regularly, we all need regular, meaningful attention—validation that we are loved, that someone cares, that we make a difference. Without that knowing, we become lethargic and lost, and we lose hope. When we think that no one cares, it often shows. It is easy to put on a tough exterior and give the appearance that we don't care, but deep down it can be pretty lonely on our own.

The basic need to be loved is universal among people and animals. Pets fill that need and do it unconditionally. No matter the day, our relationship, or our status, our pets love us anyway. That's why we enjoy them so much and why they're often used in therapy. There's something soothing about petting a happy fur ball.

I showed Keiko attention, and just when I needed it, she was right there. One time I sat on the floor on the receiving end of an unhappy, accusatory discussion. I knew that sitting on the floor put me at a lower level, often viewed as weak or submissive, but I wanted to just sit down. I didn't want this right in my face.

Keiko walked in and sat right in front of me, like a bodyguard. She sat straight up, erect, and looked straight ahead at the person handing out the argument. As the situation continued to decline, Keiko climbed into my lap and sat there. A sense of peace came over me when she did that. It was like an old friend saying, "I'm here for you." Somehow she knew just what I needed and was there for me.

Stop and think right now: Where can you show some attention that would make a difference? Where have you taken someone/a pet for granted? Write a thank you note, make a phone call, bring home dinner, turn off the TV, etc. Take a few minutes out of your day and give some love. Just a few minutes is all it takes. You'll be surprised how alive someone will feel. Guess what, so will you!!!

Unconditional love isn't always easy:

Keiko loved to be held and welcomed a good petting. As soon as I picked her up, the purr box fired up. I'd sit on the couch and here she'd come. She loved to sleep in the bed on the pillows near my head.

As the cancer continued, her appearance degraded severely. She went from a princess to an alley cat almost overnight. Aside from her looking rough, the smell of decaying flesh was sickening. I could literally smell her from across the room. It wasn't a tolerable smell; it would almost make me sick. I couldn't imagine her living with that smell all the time.

I'd give her baths almost every week to clean her up and give her some dignity. She was given baths as a kitten, so she was OK with them.

You remember how I said I'd spend more time with her? That became very difficult as the disease progressed. The sickening smell, the drool, and the wet fur made it hard to be near her, let alone pet her.

Whenever she came up to me, there was always a puddle or mark left from her drooling on me or rubbing against me. Anything she laid on or was near captured that smell.

Then one day I looked at her, and she just looked so pitiful. How could I not show this cat who'd been with me eighteen years some love? That was just being selfish and mean. I grabbed some old towels and began to hold her frequently. She just loved it. As soon as I picked her up, she'd just purr away. Yeah, the stink would get through onto my clothes, but that was OK. It was worth it.

The more I held her, the more she'd come back and rub on my legs. Oh no, here come's smelly cat!!

It had always been easy to hold her when she was clean. Now that she was stinky and sick was when she needed that affection the most. As much as I loved my cat, there were days where it was difficult to be close to her. Often I'd get upset with her, and I knew that it was my frustration coming out. I just wanted to help her be well.

Unconditional love can be hard sometimes. You have to go way past the funky appearance and the odd smells, and think solely about the other person. You have to think about what it'd be like if you were in that situation. What would you really like?

You wouldn't want to be denied affection or care because you smelled or looked funny, would you? It's those times when you need someone the most. If you've ever been to a nursing home, you'll know exactly what I mean. It's hard and sad at the same time.

 To wrap up this section, if you're feeling dull, lost, without motivation, or just depressed, get out and do something. It's very likely you've quit doing something you enjoy. For me, it was the constant exploration, the learning that occurs from experiencing new things. It could be the same for you or something totally different. Find your passion and begin doing what you enjoy. You'll become more vibrant and alive in a short time. Whatever you do, keep exploring and growing.

As you keep learning, remember to give other people and pets your attention. You may not think a simple smile is much, but it often will make someone's day. I know being told thank you is always welcomed. The more attention you give, the more alive the people and pets will become. Imagine if we all did that to each other, how much more alive we'd all be!!

And finally, remember to apply unconditional love, even when it's hard. When it's the most difficult is when it's most needed. Why wait till its difficult though? Why wait till someone is in a nursing home, a car accident, sick or lost their job? Show unconditional love, starting right now.

In conclusion:

All of those great lessons came just from observing my pets and having an encounter with sea turtles. We and the animals are much more alike than different. As you go through your life, pay attention to your animal encounters. Pay attention to their behaviors, and see what you glean from watching them. Their actions might be just what you need to see.

Just remember to see events as they are rather than making unnecessary, stressful situations out of them. Whatever you're up to, visualize your goal and keep digging. You may get some crap on you now and then, but it's worth it.

As things get tough or don't go as planned, remember those baby sea turtles. No matter what, they went to the ocean. They made it, even if it required a little help from above.

Maintain your vibrancy by continuing to learn new things and explore. Learn to dance, play music, and take a photography class. Go see something different in your own town, or go far and explore the world.

And finally, remember that sometimes you have to climb that fence. Under or around just isn't feasible. If that is your journey, make adjustments as needed and enjoy the trip. Whatever "fences" you may encounter along the way, just remember Edmund. Climb that Fence and take that Leap. It's so worth it!

Made in the USA
Charleston, SC
23 March 2013